GLOBAL**HOT**SPOTS

ZIMBABWE

Yvonne Thorpe

Marshall Cavendish
Benchmark

New York

Website: www.marshallcavendish.us

This publication represents the opinions and views of the author based on Yvonne Thorpe's personal
experience, knowledge, and research. The information in this book serves as a general guide only. The author
and publisher have used their best efforts in preparing this book and disclaim liability rising directly and
indirectly from the use and application of this book.

Other Marshall Cavendish Offices:
Marshall Cavendish Ltd. 5th Floor, 32-38 Saffron Hill, London EC1N 8 FH, UK • Marshall Cavendish International
(Asia) Private Limited, 1 New Industrial Road, Singapore 536196 • Marshall Cavendish International (Thailand)
Co Ltd. 253 Asoke, 12th Flr, Sukhumvit 21 Road, Klongtoey Nua, Wattana, Bangkok 10110, Thailand • Marshall
Cavendish (Malaysia) Sdn Bhd, Times Subang, Lot 46, Subang Hi-Tech Industrial Park, Batu Tiga, 40000 Shah
Alam, Selangor Darul Ehsan, Malaysia

Marshall Cavendish is a trademark of Times Publishing Limited

All websites were available and accurate when this book was sent to press.

Library of Congress Cataloging-in-Publication Data

Thorpe, Yvonne.
    Zimbabwe / Yvonne Thorpe.
        p. cm. — (Global hotspots)
    Includes index.
    Summary: "Discusses Zimbabwe, its history, conflicts, and the reasons why it is currently in the news"—
Provided by publisher.
    ISBN 978-0-7614-4763-4
    1. Zimbabwe—Juvenile literature. I. Thorpe, Yvonne. II. Title.
    DT2889.D68 2011
968.91—dc22
                                2009039848

First published in 2010 by
MACMILLAN EDUCATION AUSTRALIA PTY LTD
15–19 Claremont Street, South Yarra 3141

Visit our website at www.macmillan.com.au or go directly to www.macmillanlibrary.com.au

Associated companies and representatives throughout the world.

Copyright © Macmillan Education Australia 2010

 Produced for Macmillan Education Australia by
MONKEY PUZZLE MEDIA LTD
48 York Avenue, Hove BN3 1PJ, UK

Edited by Susie Brooks
Text and cover design by Tom Morris and James Winrow
Page layout by Tom Morris
Photo research by Susie Brooks and Lynda Lines
Maps by Martin Darlison, Encompass Graphics

Printed in the United States

Acknowledgments
The author and the publisher are grateful to the following for permission to reproduce copyright material:

Front cover photograph: Zimbabwean riot police fire teargas at students during a peaceful march in the capital, Harare.
Courtesy of Reuters (Howard Burditt).

Corbis, **10** (Bettmann), **13** (Bettmann), **14** (Hulton-Deutsch Collection), **15** (Hulton-Deutsch Collection), **19** (Gideon Mendel),
21 (Gideon Mendel), **22** (Gideon Mendel), **24** (Gideon Mendel), **25** (Gideon Mendel), **26** (epa), **29** (Aaron Ufumeli); Getty
Images, **4**, **20** (AFP), **23** (AFP), **27**, **28** (AFP); iStockphoto, **30**; MPM Images, **6** (Jan Derk), **8**; Topfoto.co.uk, **7** (The Granger
Collection), **11** (AP), **12** (AP), **16**, **18** (AP).

While every care has been taken to trace and acknowledge copyright, the publisher tenders their apologies for any
accidental infringement where copyright has proved untraceable. Where the attempt has been unsuccessful, the
publisher welcomes information that would redress the situation.

1 3 5 6 4 2

CONTENTS

Glossary Words

When a word is printed in **bold**, you can look up its meaning in the Glossary on page 31.

ALWAYS IN THE NEWS

Global hot spots are places that are always in the news. They are places where there has been conflict between different groups of people for years. Sometimes the conflicts have lasted for hundreds of years.

Why Do Hot Spots Happen?

There are four main reasons why hot spots happen:

1 Disputes over land, and who has the right to live on it.

2 Disagreements over religion and **culture**, where different peoples find it impossible to live happily side-by-side.

3 Arguments over how the government should be organized.

4 Conflict over resources, such as oil, gold, or diamonds.

Sometimes these disagreements spill over into violence—and into the headlines.

HOT SPOT BRIEFING

KEY ISSUES IN ZIMBABWE
Today, Zimbabwe's people face four key problems:
1 The country's economy is in ruins.
2 Zimbabwe no longer produces enough food to feed its people.
3 Many Zimbabweans feel that their government does not represent their views.
4 The deadly **HIV/AIDS** virus affects many people.

Desperate Zimbabweans seek help at a refugee center in South Africa. By 2008, when this photo was taken, life in Zimbabwe had become so hard that millions of people had left their country.

Zimbabwe

Zimbabwe is a country in southern Africa. Most of its people come from two African **tribes**, the Shona and the Ndebele. There are also a few Zimbabweans who are the descendants of settlers from Europe.

Zimbabwe as a Hot Spot

Zimbabwe has been in the news a lot recently. Zimbabwe's leader, Robert Mugabe, used violence and torture against people who opposed his rule. Ordinary people's lives became harder and harder. Millions of them left the country and became **exiles**. Today, the growing number of exiles is proof of Zimbabwe's problems.

"Everything is gone and the children are not getting enough food... They go to school barefoot with torn clothes [and] I can't find even one **rand** to buy them books or pencils."

Idah Mbizvo, a Zimbabwean villager, February 2009.

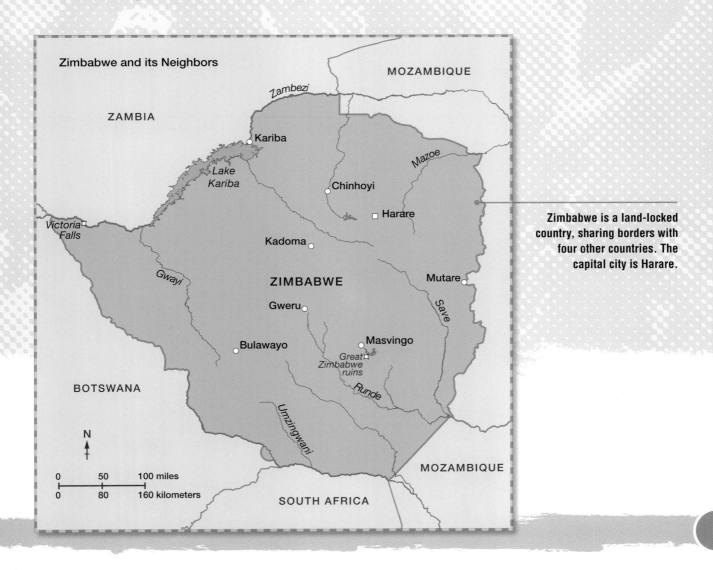

Zimbabwe and its Neighbors

MOZAMBIQUE

ZAMBIA

Zambezi

Kariba

Mazoe

Lake Kariba

Chinhoyi

Harare

Victoria Falls

Kadoma

Gwayi

ZIMBABWE

Mutare

Gweru

Save

Masvingo

Bulawayo

Great Zimbabwe ruins

BOTSWANA

Runde

Umzingwani

N

| 0 | 50 | 100 miles |
| 0 | 80 | 160 kilometers |

MOZAMBIQUE

SOUTH AFRICA

Zimbabwe is a land-locked country, sharing borders with four other countries. The capital city is Harare.

AN ANCIENT CIVILIZATION

Zimbabwe was once at the heart of a great **civilization** in southern Africa. Almost a thousand years ago, Zimbabweans were building great cities, and trading with foreign countries far away.

Great Zimbabwe

The ancient, ruined city of Great Zimbabwe is one of the most famous reminders of Zimbabwe's history. The Shona people built it, some time after 1000 CE. The builders used a building technique that was special because it involved fitting huge stone slabs together without **mortar**.

"There is a fortress built of stones of marvelous size ... one tower [is] more than 12 fathoms [72 feet or 22 meters] high."

Portuguese soldier Vicente Pegado, describing Great Zimbabwe in 1531.

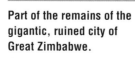
Part of the remains of the gigantic, ruined city of Great Zimbabwe.

A Shona Empire

Between the 1400s and the early 1800s, Shona people ruled over a large **empire** in southern Africa. It included most of what is now Zimbabwe. The empire's ivory, gold, and copper were traded far away. Porcelain from China, and cloth and beads from Indonesia were brought into the empire.

Arrival of the Ndebele

During the 1830s, a people called the Ndebele began to arrive in Zimbabwe. They had been driven from their old territory by a fearsome Zulu leader, Shaka, and his warriors. Within a few years, the Ndebele had conquered the Shona and controlled most of Zimbabwe.

HOT SPOT BRIEFING

SHAKA
Shaka was the ruler of the Zulu people from 1816 to 1828. Shaka perfected new battle tactics and fighting methods, which for a while made his armies almost invincible. Using these, Shaka led a huge expansion of Zulu territory.

This engraving from an English newspaper in 1879 shows a Zulu attack. Zulu warriors drove the Ndebele people from their homelands and into Zimbabwe in the 1830s.

THE COLONIAL ERA

In the late 1800s, British traders began to take control of large areas of southern Africa. These areas eventually became British **colonies**, and among them was Zimbabwe.

This cartoon shows Cecil Rhodes standing across all of Africa. His power did not actually extend across the entire continent, but he controlled large areas of southern Africa, including what would become Zimbabwe.

British Power Grows

Between 1888 and 1897, the British became increasingly powerful in Zimbabwe. An adventurer named Cecil Rhodes persuaded the king of the Ndebele to give Rhodes's British South Africa Company (BSAC) permission to start mining in the area. The BSAC, backed by its armed police force, steadily took over the government of the region.

HOT SPOT BRIEFING

CECIL RHODES
Cecil Rhodes was one of Britain's most successful and ruthless empire builders. Having made a fortune in diamond mining, he oversaw a huge expansion of British territory in southern Africa. Botswana, Zimbabwe and Zambia all became British colonies as a result of Rhodes's actions.

Rhodesia

In 1895, the southern African territory controlled by the BSAC was named Rhodesia. The land that is now Zimbabwe became Southern Rhodesia. At this time, many white European settlers came to the region. They built farms and began to grow crops, usually on land that had belonged to black Africans.

A British Colony

In 1923, Southern Rhodesia became a British colony, part of the British Empire. It remained a colony until 1965. The tiny white **minority**, which was less than 5 percent of the population, continued to govern the whole country.

HOT SPOT BRIEFING

REVOLTS AGAINST THE BSAC
There were two major revolts against the growing power of the BSAC (British South Africa Company), in 1893–1894 and 1896–1897. Cecil Rhodes and the BSAC crushed the revolts, and used them as an excuse to take complete control of the region.

This map shows the territories of Northern Rhodesia (now mainly Zambia) and Southern Rhodesia (now Zimbabwe).

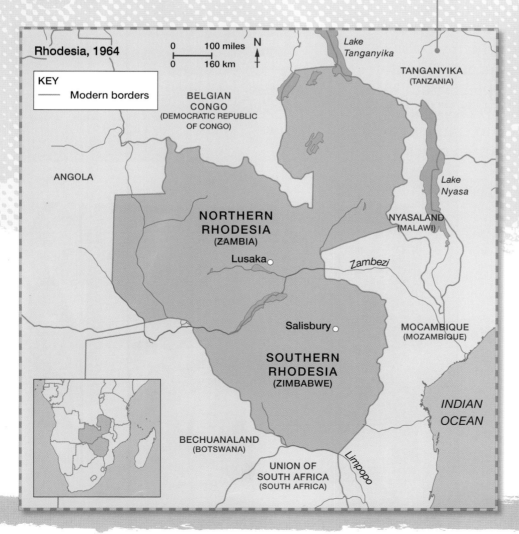

Rhodesia, 1964

0   100 miles
0   160 km

N

KEY
— Modern borders

BELGIAN CONGO (DEMOCRATIC REPUBLIC OF CONGO)

ANGOLA

Lake Tanganyika

TANGANYIKA (TANZANIA)

Lake Nyasa

NORTHERN RHODESIA (ZAMBIA)

Lusaka

Zambezi

NYASALAND (MALAWI)

Salisbury

MOCAMBIQUE (MOZAMBIQUE)

SOUTHERN RHODESIA (ZIMBABWE)

INDIAN OCEAN

BECHUANALAND (BOTSWANA)

Limpopo

UNION OF SOUTH AFRICA (SOUTH AFRICA)

INDEPENDENCE

In 1965, Southern Rhodesia became independent, like many African countries at the time. Unlike most places, however, independence in Southern Rhodesia was not good news for its black people.

Independence Declared

Independence was declared by Prime Minister Ian Smith, leader of Rhodesia's whites-only government, not by Britain. Smith's aim was to stop the British from allowing black Rhodesians to vote, which would have ended complete control of the country by white people. Britain said that Smith's actions were illegal, and immediately refused to trade with Rhodesia. Other countries quickly followed suit.

HOT SPOT BRIEFING

SANCTIONS
In 1966, the **United Nations (UN)** called for its members to observe **sanctions** against Rhodesia, including:
- An **embargo** on buying 90 percent of Rhodesia's products
- A call for UN members not to sell oil, weapons, motor vehicles, or aircraft to Rhodesia

In 1965, Prime Minister Ian Smith signs the declaration of independence, watched by Rhodesian officials.

Civil War

By the early 1970s, a **civil war** had begun in Rhodesia. On one side, determined to hang on to power for as long as possible, were the Smith government and the army. On the other, demanding that black people should have the same rights as whites, were the forces of Joshua Nkomo's ZAPU party and Robert Mugabe's ZANU party.

Guerrilla War

ZAPU and ZANU fought a **guerrilla** war. They began by attacking isolated white-owned farms. Soon, though, the guerrillas were attacking roads, railways, factories, and security posts. They gradually wore the Smith government down. By 1978, the government was on the brink of collapse.

HOT SPOT BRIEFING

ZAPU AND ZANU
The two main resistance groups in Rhodesia in the 1970s were ZAPU and ZANU.
- ZAPU stood for Zimbabwe African People's Union. ZAPU was formed in 1961, and had Shona and Ndebele members.
- ZANU stood for Zimbabwe African National Union. ZANU was formed from a breakaway group of ZAPU members in 1963, and from 1975 onward was mainly a Shona party.

Members of the fighting arm of ZANU, which fought a guerrilla war against the Rhodesian government, display their weapons.

1978–1979: ELECTIONS

By the late 1970s, Ian Smith realized that he would not be able to stay in power for much longer. He decided to try and reach an agreement with carefully chosen black leaders.

The Internal Settlement

In March 1978, an "Internal Settlement" was signed between the Smith government and some black leaders. The Settlement allowed black people to vote in elections, but placed strict limits on what power they would have.

ZAPU and ZANU react

ZAPU and ZANU refused to support the Internal Settlement. They pointed out that the Settlement meant that white people would keep many of their privileges. The guerrilla war against the government continued.

HOT SPOT BRIEFING

INTERNAL SETTLEMENT
The key agreements reached under the Internal Settlement included:
- Whites would control the police, **civil service**, defense forces, and legal system.
- Whites would control about a third of the seats in **parliament**.
- Blacks could now vote.

Members of the armed resistance to Rhodesia's whites-only government gather in January 1979, near the border with Mozambique.

1979 Elections

In 1979, Rhodesia held its first elections in which blacks and whites could both vote. The United African National Council (UANC) party won, and a government of mainly black leaders was formed. The new prime minister was a black bishop called Abel Muzorewa.

Election Rejection

Many people in Rhodesia and overseas rejected the election results. In Zimbabwe, many black people felt that the new government did not represent their views. ZAPU and ZANU carried on their attacks on government forces. Other countries around the world refused to recognize Bishop Muzorewa's government, and sanctions continued.

> "I don't believe in black majority rule in Rhodesia. Not in a thousand years."
>
> Rhodesian Prime Minister Ian Smith, March 1976.

Supporters of Bishop Abel Muzorewa campaign for his victory in the Rhodesian elections of April 1979.

TALKS IN LONDON

After the elections of 1979, Rhodesia was renamed Zimbabwe-Rhodesia. Little else changed. ZAPU and ZANU were still fighting a guerrilla war, and other countries did not accept the new government.

1979 London Meetings

In late 1979, the British government invited all of Zimbabwe-Rhodesia's leaders to talks in Lancaster House, London. Everyone hoped that the talks would result in a solution to Zimbabwe's problems, and allow the civil war to end. On one side were ZANU and ZAPU, on the other were Bishop Muzorewa and Ian Smith.

Zimbabwean leaders Robert Mugabe (on the left) and Joshua Nkomo attend the Lancaster House conference.

HOT SPOT BRIEFING

LINKS WITH BRITAIN
Why did Britain host the meetings between Zimbabwe-Rhodesia's leaders in 1979?
- In theory, Zimbabwe was still part of the British Empire, because its 1965 declaration of independence had not been recognized by other countries.
- Many farms and businesses there were owned by British companies.
- Many white Zimbabweans had British passports.

MR. R.C. MUGABE

Land Reform

Land ownership, or **land reform**, was a crunch issue at the London talks. Robert Mugabe, in particular, argued that white-owned farms were on land that had once belonged to black people, and had to be given back. The other side argued that many farms had been white-owned for generations, so their owners should keep them.

In the end it was agreed that some land reform would take place. Britain and the United States both offered to help white farmers who lost their land.

White farming families are trained to use guns in May 1979. Many white Zimbabweans feared they would be attacked by black Zimbabweans if the whites lost power.

A Final Agreement

Zimbabwe's leaders signed the Lancaster House Agreement on December 1, 1979. The Agreement replaced the Internal Settlement, giving Zimbabwe-Rhodesia a new **constitution**. It ended the civil war by promising elections in which blacks and whites would have equal votes, and was recognized by governments around the world.

HOT SPOT BRIEFING

INTERNATIONAL RELATIONS
After Lancaster House, Zimbabwe-Rhodesia was once more part of the international community.
- Trade restrictions ended, so the country's businesses could buy and sell goods overseas.
- Aid for the poorest people began to flow into the country. More than $985 million was promised at the talks.

MUGABE TAKES POWER

In 1980, ZAPU and ZANU **disbanded** their armies. Zimbabwe finally became legally independent from Britain, and in February the country's first elections under the new constitution were held.

Mugabe's Election Victory

The results of the 1980 elections were victory for Robert Mugabe and the ZANU party. The security forces, which were dominated by whites, had tried to bully people into voting for Bishop Muzorewa's party. It had not worked, and Mugabe swept to power with a huge victory.

"If you were my enemy, you are now my friend. If you hated me, you cannot avoid the love that binds me to you and you to me."

Robert Mugabe, after Zimbabwe had become independent.

Supporters of Robert Mugabe wear the cockerel symbol of Robert Mugabe's party on their T-shirts at a 1980 election rally.

Opposition in Matabeleland

In Matabeleland, where most Ndebele people lived, there was opposition to the ZANU victory. Most ZANU members were Shona people. The Ndebele were not happy that the Shona had so much power. In late 1980 and early 1981, there were uprisings against the ZANU government.

Securing Power

Between 1982 and 1987, President Mugabe and ZANU moved to get rid of opposition to their rule:

- In Matabeleland, more than 20,000 Ndebele are thought to have been killed by pro-Mugabe forces. These killings became known as the Matabeleland Massacres.

- In 1987, ZANU and ZAPU agreed to merge. They joined together as ZANU-PF (the PF stands for Patriotic Front).

By the late 1980s, Mugabe and ZANU-PF had near-complete control of Zimbabwe.

"This was a barbaric operation by [ZANU]. It should never have happened. It was a sad episode in our history and ... those responsible will have to account for their actions."

Opposition leader, Morgan Tsvangirai, speaking in 2001 about the Matabeleland Massacres.

Matabeleland

Matabeleland is in the west of Zimbabwe and is divided into North and South. The major city is Bulawayo.

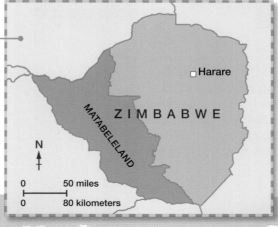

1990s: DECADE OF CHANGE

After the turmoil of the 1970s and 1980s, many Zimbabweans hoped life would finally begin to improve. Life did get better for some, but many others were unhappy about the way ZANU-PF was running the country.

Presidents Robert Mugabe and Nelson Mandela of South Africa shake hands in 1990, as they celebrate ten years of Zimbabwean independence. President Mugabe had just been re-elected, with four of every five Zimbabweans who voted supporting him.

1990 Elections

In 1990, elections were held. The results seemed to be a big success for ZANU-PF. The party won all but three of the seats in parliament, and President Mugabe was re-elected with a huge victory. But only about half of Zimbabweans had voted. The rest either were not interested in the elections, or did not want to support ZANU-PF.

1990 ELECTION STATISTICS

STATISTICS

- Fifty-four percent of people voted.
- ZANU-PF won 85 percent of the vote, and 117 of 120 seats in parliament.
- In the presidential elections held at the same time, Robert Mugabe won 80 percent of the votes.

Anti-government Protests

Throughout the 1990s, there were protests against the ZANU-PF government. People were increasingly unhappy at the way President Mugabe refused to allow any opposition to his rule. They were also unhappy at the rising prices of goods, especially in cities. As a result, there were student protests, and strikes by **civil servants**, doctors and nurses.

Improvements

The 1990s saw big improvements in some areas of Zimbabwean life, especially the economy. By the late 1990s:

- Zimbabwe's goods and services were worth a third more than in the 1980s.
- The country was **self-sufficient** in food, and exported more than 1.5 million tons of maize and 260,000 tons of tobacco each year.
- More than 90 percent of Zimbabweans were able to read and write.

Buyers examine crates of dried tobacco before an auction in Harare in 1993. Tobacco was one of Zimbabwe's most valuable crops, and brought in millions of dollars a year.

"People are leaving Zimbabwe because the government is not looking after the people – it's against the people, it's beating people, it's shooting people."

A Zimbabwean exile explains why he felt he had to leave the country.

HIV IN ZIMBABWE

During the 1990s, the deadly HIV virus began to spread among Zimbabweans. Today it has become one of the greatest problems faced by the country, with one in ten Zimbabweans suffering from it.

AIDS

AIDS is an illness caused by the HIV virus. There is no cure. The virus stops the body from fighting off diseases. The problem gets worse and worse until the patient develops AIDS. People with AIDS cannot fight off even minor illnesses, and soon die.

HIV/AIDS STATISTICS

STATISTICS

In a 2008 United Nations report, figures showed that:

- Zimbabwe had the world's sixth-largest population of people living with HIV/AIDS—1.3 million of a total population of 11.3 million.
- Just over 15 percent of all 15- to 49-year old Zimbabweans had HIV.
- 140,000 Zimbabweans had died of AIDS that year.
- One million Zimbabwean children had been orphaned by AIDS.

Children whose parents have died of AIDS attend a special camp during the school holidays in 2004.

The Spread of HIV/AIDS

HIV/AIDS has spread far and wide among Zimbabweans. There are three main reasons for this:

1 Because ordinary Zimbabweans did not know about HIV/AIDS, it was able to spread quickly.

2 The government refused to face the problem, and did not tell people how to avoid being infected.

3 Drugs called **ARVs** can slow the development of the virus, but many people did not get them.

Partly because of the spread of HIV/AIDS, Zimbabwe's average **life expectancy** is now around 40 years—one of the lowest in the world.

Hunger and HIV/AIDS

Today, food shortages mean that many Zimbabweans do not get enough to eat. This means that their bodies are weak and lack energy. They are even less able to resist the HIV virus, so they risk developing AIDS and dying very quickly.

Although Zimbabwe does receive help from other countries, its government can be hostile toward aid organizations, which limits the help available.

"It's all down to food. Without food, AIDS comes, **cholera** comes. The weak [people] die. Any disease, they die."

A Zimbabwean health worker, 2009.

By 2000, when this AIDS rally took place, a high percentage of young Zimbabweans had HIV / AIDS. The government was unable to provide the special ARV drugs that could keep them alive.

LAND REFORM

From the late 1990s onward, land reform became one of the biggest issues in Zimbabwean politics. President Mugabe used land reform to try to increase his declining popularity.

Unequal Ownership

President Mugabe said that Zimbabwe's current land ownership was unequal. He claimed that whites made up 1 percent of the population, but still owned 70 percent of farmland. Because food was Zimbabwe's main export, this meant that whites controlled most of the country's income from overseas.

"Our fathers fought the white man in the 1950s so they could take over their land, but foreigners today continue to occupy large farms while our people remain landless."

Stephen Ndicho of the Kenyan Social Democratic Party, supporting seizures of white-owned farms in Africa in 2000.

A Zimbabwean farmer watches the harvest of his tobacco crop.

Farm Seizures

In the late 1990s, Zimbabwe's government began allowing its supporters to seize white-owned farms. Sometimes the seizures were made under a government plan to give white-owned farms to black Zimbabweans. Sometimes raiders illegally seized the farms, often using violence. The police said it would be impossible to remove them. By 2008, very few Zimbabwean farms remained in white ownership.

Purpose of the Seizures

The government argued that the farm seizures were a way of making life fairer for all Zimbabweans. The government's opponents pointed out that much of the land had been given to government supporters. Government ministers themselves now own some of the biggest farms.

HOT SPOT BRIEFING

THE WAR VETERANS ASSOCIATION
The War Veterans Association led the seizures of white-owned farms.
- Its members had all fought in the civil war of the 1970s.
- "War vets" were still willing to use violence to get their way.
- The Association had close links to ZANU-PF, campaigning for the party in elections.

These Zimbabweans seized a white-owned farm in 2000. Many farms across the country were occupied by veterans of the war of independence, who were determined to grab a piece of land that they could farm.

ZIMBABWE IN CRISIS

Within a few years, it became clear that the land reforms that started in the 1990s had not been a success. In fact, they plunged Zimbabwe further into crisis.

Unproductive Farmland

After the farm seizures, much of Zimbabwe's farmland became far less productive. Each year, the **yields** from the country's farms fell. The problems were made worse by a **drought** in southern Africa, which affected even the few productive farms that remained. Food shortages became common, and the price of food increased hugely.

HOT SPOT BRIEFING

FARM FAILURES
Why did Zimbabwe's farms fail after the land reforms?
- The land was split into small "parcels," which meant that large-scale farming methods could no longer be used.
- The new landowners did not have much money, so they could not afford machinery, seeds, and fertilizers.
- The new owners often knew little or nothing about farming.

In October 2002, the new owner of formerly white-owned farmland plows the soil using oxen. Like this man, many black farmers lacked the technology to make their land profitable.

Rising Prices

As agriculture declined, the cost of many products, not only food, began to rise. Sales of tobacco and maize to other countries had once brought in money from overseas. Zimbabwe needed this money to buy imported goods such as gasoline and machinery. Without it, the prices of imported goods rose daily.

Rising Unpopularity

As prices rose, people became more unhappy with President Mugabe's government. In 2000, the Movement for Democratic Change (MDC) was formed to protest the government's handling of affairs. The police and army cracked down violently on any opposition, which made the government even less popular.

"There's no law in Zimbabwe. The law is for the president, he works for himself with the police and army only. That's why people are running away from Zimbabwe."

Christopher, who left Zimbabwe for South Africa in 2007.

By December 2002, gasoline had become hard to find (and very expensive) in Zimbabwe. This line of cars and vans was hoping to fill up with gasoline in Harare.

ELECTION BATTLES

By 2007, President Mugabe's government was unpopular with all but his closest supporters. In March 2008, parliamentary and presidential elections gave Zimbabweans the chance to take action.

Opposition leader Morgan Tsvangirai votes in the March 2008 presidential elections, in which he gained more votes than Robert Mugabe. However, Mugabe refused to give up the presidency.

March Elections

In the March elections, MDC leader Morgan Tsvangirai won 47.8 percent of the vote. This was more than President Mugabe's 43.2 percent. The MDC also won more parliamentary seats than any other party. But to be elected president, Tsvangirai needed more than 50 percent of the vote. A second presidential election was scheduled.

HOT SPOT BRIEFING

2008 CHOLERA EPIDEMIC
In August 2008, Zimbabwe's problems became worse when the country was hit by a cholera epidemic. By February 2009:
• At least 12,545 cases had been reported.
• At least 565 people had died.
The true numbers were thought to be much higher, but information from isolated rural parts of Zimbabwe was not available.

Campaign of Violence

Before the March elections, government supporters had begun a campaign of violence against the MDC. MDC leaders were arrested, beaten, or killed. Its election meetings were disrupted or banned. In the time before the second presidential election, the violence and threats became even worse. Finally, Morgan Tsvangirai was forced to withdraw.

Power-sharing

The results of the March election forced President Mugabe to promise to share power with the MDC. The promise was an empty one, and for the rest of the year he kept control of the government and armed forces. By the end of 2008, though, other countries were calling for harsher sanctions against Zimbabwe. They hoped to force Mugabe to make a deal with the MDC.

"People are dying in hospitals and funeral expenses are very high, how do you expect us to survive? Shop shelves are empty. If we vote, things might get back to normal."

Gertrude Muzanenhamo, Harare, March 2008.

Protesters in London, England, demonstrate in June 2008 against Mugabe's rule of Zimbabwe.

ZIMBABWE'S CHALLENGES

By early 2009, the situation for many Zimbabweans had become unbearable, and millions of people had left the country. But it also seemed that there might be some hope for a better future.

A New Prime Minister

On February 10, 2009, Morgan Tsvangirai became Zimbabwe's new prime minister, with Robert Mugabe remaining president. The MDC had agreed to a temporary power-sharing deal, and aimed to hold new elections within two years. The MDC expects that these will result in Morgan Tsvangirai becoming president.

Mugabe and ZANU-PF

President Mugabe and ZANU-PF do not seem likely to give up power easily. ZANU-PF members still control key parts of the government, the police, and the army. They had already shown that they were willing to break the law and use violence against their opponents.

Zimbabweans salute their new prime minister, Morgan Tsvangirai, on February 11, 2009. Tsvangirai had just been sworn in by President Mugabe.

Challenges Ahead

By the time Morgan Tsvangirai became prime minister, the challenges Zimbabwe faced were huge:

- Zimbabwe's **currency** was worthless. Without Zimbabwean money, it became difficult for people to buy food and other goods. The government struggled to pay its employees.
- School teachers and doctors were no longer being paid, leading many schools and hospitals to close.
- Roads and sewers were breaking apart and becoming unusable.
- Four out of every five people were unemployed.
- The 2009 harvest was the worst in thirty years.

Hope for the Future

Zimbabweans have already lived through difficult times and survived. Their toughness and determination should help them to rebuild their country. Morgan Tsvangirai is working on plans to revive Zimbabwe's currency, which would mean employees could be paid and the country could get back on its feet.

> "The MDC cannot be authors of chaos by allowing the country to go over the precipice."

Morgan Tsvangirai explains why the MDC decided to share power with Robert Mugabe.

By January 2009, Zimbabwe's currency was worth so little that the government began to print these ZWL$10 trillion notes. The people needed this much money for even small purchases, such as eggs.

FACTFINDER: Zimbabwe

Full Name Republic of Zimbabwe

Capital Harare

Area 150,804 square miles
(390,580 square kilometers)

Population 11,392,629 (July 2009 estimate)

Rate of population change 1.53% per year
(2009 estimate)

Industries Mining, steel, wood products, cement

Gross Domestic Product* per person US$200
(2008 estimate)

Percentage of labor force in agriculture 66%
(1997)

Percentage of labor force in industry 10%
(1997)

Percentage of labor force in services 24%
(1997)

Number of phone lines 344,500 (2007)

Number of TV stations 16 (in 2008)

NOTE: In 2009, unemployment in Zimbabwe was estimated to be about 90 percent. The cost of goods was estimated to be rising by 11,200,000 percent a year.

> * Gross Domestic Product, or GDP, is the value of all the goods and services produced by a country in a year. (Source for statistics: *CIA World Factbook*)

The flag of Zimbabwe

FOCUS QUESTIONS

These questions might help you to think about some of the issues raised in *Zimbabwe*.

Leadership and Government

How did being in the British Empire affect Zimbabwe?
How have Zimbabwe's various leaders ruled the country?

Economy

How did becoming independent affect Zimbabwe's economy?

Politics

Does Zimbabwe's government have good relations with other countries, in Africa and elsewhere?
How have the leaders of other countries tried to affect the government of Zimbabwe?

Citizenship

Have Zimbabwe's recent elections resulted in a government that most people support?
Why have millions of Zimbabweans left the country?

GLOSSARY

AIDS Acquired Immunodeficiency Syndrome, a disease that stops the body from fighting off illnesses

ARVs antiretrovirals, drugs that can slow down the progress of the HIV virus

cholera infectious disease of the digestive system, which often causes death

civil service government departments and their employees, called civil servants

civil war war between different groups within their own country

civilization society that has developed its own culture

colonies countries ruled by another country

constitution set of rules stating how a country will be governed

culture things that make a society or people distinctive, such as their language, clothes, food, music, songs, and stories

currency money, particular to a certain country, for example the United States dollar

disband break up or stop using

drought period of unusually dry weather, in which water becomes scarce

embargo restriction on trade

empire large group of countries ruled by a single country

exiles people who have left or been forced to leave their own country

guerrilla hit-and-run fighter, often one who aims to overthrow a government

HIV Human Immunodeficiency Virus, a virus that causes the killer disease AIDS

land reform changes in the ownership of land

life expectancy how long a person can expect, on average, to live

minority smaller group within a larger group or population

mortar paste that, when dry, holds together bricks or rocks to make a wall

parliament group of members or representatives of a political nation

rand South African currency

sanctions restrictions or penalties, threatened or carried out as punishment

self-sufficient able to provide for one's own needs without help from others

tribe group of people with a common language and traditions

United Nations organization set up after World War II that aims to help countries end disputes without fighting

yield amount of crop produced

INDEX